WHATEVER HAPPENED TO LOVE

By
James Newkirk

Copyright @2019 By James Newkirk

All rights reserved. No part of this publication may be reproduced, stored in a retrieval system, or transmitted in any form or by any means electronic, mechanical, photocopying, recording, or otherwise without the written permission of the authors.

Limits of Liability-Disclaimer

The authors and publisher shall not be liable for your misuse of this material. The purpose of this book is to educate and empower. The authors and/or publisher do not guarantee that anyone following these techniques, suggestions, tips, ideas, and/or strategies will become successful.

The authors and/or publisher shall have neither liability nor responsibility to anyone with respect to any loss or damage caused or alleged to be caused directly or indirectly by the information contained in this book.

TABLE OF CONTENTS

Dedication i

Introduction 1

CHAPTER 1: *Stuck on Stupid* 3

CHAPTER 2: *I forgive you* 10

CHAPTER 3: Have you ever 16

CHAPTER 4: *I QUIT!!! (The Dating Game)* 20

CHAPTER 5: *So what happens now?* 32

CHAPTER 6: *Communication* 36

CHAPTER 7: *A Ray of hope* 43

About the Author 47

DEDICATION

To my family, thank you for always believing in me. For being there when I needed you the most. Even when I wanted to put the pen down you encouraged me to go farther.

To Vanessa, Natasha, and Dr. Finch, who've known meeting you three for the first time would change my life so drastically, I am glad to call you my sisters.

To Stefan: Thank you for showing me how to love, accept love, and giving love. Without you, I would have never discovered this part of me. R.I.P

INTRODUCTION

This book will break down the life of how many of us choose to ignore signs and wonders of a relationship, that we are so desperately seeking. Some of you will find that you are inviting tragedy into your life which will inevitably end; just like it started it will end in tragedy. You will see people that are consumed with themselves and never giving their mates a chance to get a word in edgewise. You will find the ones that complain all the time. And let's not forget about the cheaters, the ones who cheat on each other and sometimes it's both of them cheating on one another with the same person.

Love has to be the most unpredictable thing in the world. Sometimes you feel like you want it, but then the actions of others will make you look at love in an entirely different perspective.

It's not easy being with someone that makes you feel as if their life is more important than yours. Just because your life is the way you chose for it to be, and their life is the way they chose for theirs to be doesn't mean that one's life is more important than the other one. If anything, you are the stronger of the two and they will need you. Ask yourself the questions, what kind of difference has your life been since you two have been together? How have they enhanced your life? Do you find yourself happier with or were you better without them?

Everyone should take a moment to examine what type of relationship they are involved with even now. There are some signals and some signs that are unavoidable and there are some that we choose to ignore. Whatever the case is you should at least catch a few of them. Many times, we choose not to see them and that is our choice, many of them we will have to live with. Check your pulse, make sure you are alive and continue to live. Live in love, into bliss or just live alone. Either way, happiness belongs to you.

CHAPTER 1:

STUCK ON STUPID

It's not every day that you find that special someone to be in love with. To have them open up your heart, recall all your hopes, your dreams, your lifelong fulfillment, to actually restart your heart so you can begin to love again.

So, here it goes.

It was just after Thanksgiving Day I was online minding my own business and they pop in and said hello. I spoke back I was asked for my name. I asked them theirs and shortly we begin to talk. Moments later we did exchange names and phone numbers. Reluctantly enough I wasn't so willing to give them my phone number at first, but I did.

We begin to text on the phone, weeks went by so I got tired of texting and I asked them. "When do I get to hear your voice?" A few minutes later they called me and told me their name was AJ. I told him my name was Deric, but with a different spelling. We talked for a couple of weeks and then the conversation died, that should have given me a clue right there, but I wanted to know more. I texted them again ask them how they were feeling, I let them know that I miss chatting with them, they said "likewise."

Going into Christmas holiday break we talked here and there, text daily, but that was about it. I went home for Christmas break and shortly after I became sick and ended up in the hospital for a week. They were very worried about me I thought that was cute, especially for a person that I just met. Fast forward into us dating or beginning to date.

It was Wednesday before their birthday, I had found out that they have never had anyone to spend their birthday with, or to chill with. I told them I would spend this birthday with them and we did. We went out to eat, then back to their place. We laughed and talked some more and then I hugged them and then I kissed them and they kissed me back and the next thing I know we were cuddling, laying in the bed as if we've known each other for forever, clothing on of course.

We talked about our wants and our needs, told them what I expected in a relationship, and they told me what they expected in the relationship. It seems to me that we wanted the exact same thing. We wanted it from each other and no one else. We hug, kiss, cuddle like we did the day before and it felt good. I was comfortable enough to open up at this point, about my past relationships and about my spouse who has been deceased for some time.

They told me about all their relationships and all about their past experience. How often we let our guards down so fast without checking all the fact of what we need to hear? They expressed to me that they were still in touch with their exes' and that they still go to dinner, talk often and help each other out from time to time. That should have been another signal, for me to let them go. An ex is an ex for a reason, talking and going to dinner with them is not one of them.

The next day I did not go to see them because they went to hang out with their friends. My thoughts are if your friends really wanted to see you, why did they not make the effort to be in your presence for your birthday. I was determined to see them that night so I left and I went to see them. I knew that I need it to let them know everything about me and talk to them on a really serious level. We talked and they said they didn't care, but what matter is that they liked me anyway so I stayed for a little while and then I went home.

We texted each other the next morning I told them that I was thinking about them, they responded back later on and said work was really busy because they were just returning back and I told them that I understood and to call me when you get off work, they said okay. At this point, it is late in the afternoon and I could do nothing but think about them all day long so I text them again. We would text each other back and forth, we would make each other smile every time with our picture text. Eventually, I told them that, with the picture messaging

I was smiling every time I thought of them, I would get a text from them and every time I text them I would just smile, they thought I was cute. Due to our schedules, it was difficult to see each other for the next few days.

We made plans to see each other over the weekend. I was with my family and I couldn't see them, but we planned to meet, Sunday after church service. I decided to go brunch with some friends and then go see them afterward and that's exactly what happened. It was nice spending some time with them and later on went back to their house. They explained to me that they were missing me as much as I was missing them but probably more.

The funniest thing, I get so comfortable at their place and I fall asleep in their arms and I love the way it feels and I love the way they felt. We enjoyed each other company and we are happy. I don't think I've been that happy since my spouse had passed away. Once I got home I let them know that I arrived back home safely and proceeded to speak with the family. I went upstairs talk to them on the phone for a while, maybe about an hour, I know rude huh. My family was still here so I decided to stay in my room on the phone and talk to them.

At the beginning of any relationship, there will always be something to talk about, plus we still get to know one other. We expressed how we want to be inclusive to one another and looking forward to spending more time together. Suddenly, they would start calling me baby and

I would reply, who me. It was cute because it felt so natural and heartfelt. We both are on the same page in knowing what we both want and we understood we are in this together. Now we're just waiting to see what happens from here whether we connect more. At this point, I think this is going to be a serious connection.

Weeks went by, now months went by, and we fell in love. If you saw them, you would see me. Everything was going great but the people around me notice that I had completely changed, I was not myself. I was doing things out of the ordinary. I was coming in and staying out late, being tired didn't care. We going out to eat, and for some reason, I paid every time. I was running rapid but was unaware of what I was running from. But instead, I thought I was running to. It was like I was in a field of butterflies. But, little did I know I was still hurting from my pain, and trying to mask it with this new thing that I thought was love. I thought this new found relationship and now love was going to take over my heart to the point I no longer felt the pain that I was hiding.

Someone that would be there when I needed them but in reality, that thing I thought was love was not love. This thing was demanding and commanding me. It was controlling me, it was telling me to do things that I normally wouldn't do. It was showing me things that I didn't even want to see. I refer back to my book, Cries of a Broken Man and Screams of a Broken Woman. I knew what this was because I had seen it before.

This "Tin Man" was not going to ruin my life. We continued on with our relationship and I thought I could change them. That was the wrong thing for me to do because leopards never change their spots. I continued on trying to change one little thing here and another little thing there, but still no reaction.

Instead, I was adapting to them, you should never adapt, you should be the change. Especially if you're the one who needs and deserving to see a change in your own life. But needless to say, it came to a screeching halt with a phone call, from someone who was not in the relationship, and I had never met this person but had noticed my actions because actions do speak louder than words.

She told me to get it together, you're still hurting there's no reason for you to be with this person. She went on to say that, yes, I'm glad that they're here for you, for now, but this is not who you are. This is not who I have grown and known you to be. I just needed to look in the mirror, look deep down inside and find myself.

I never cried so much, it's so hard because I knew I was wrong for leading that person on. I knew deep down the entire time that I really didn't want to be with them, but they were just a cover, a cover for the pain that I was feeling inside. A cover to hide the fact that I missed the love of my life so much that I was willing to hurt someone else that really was looking for love.

I knew I had to let them go, but when I came face to face with the fact that I was also being played and strung along. Made me realize that if I had stayed, I would have been hurt even more than I was hurting now. I was shown that they didn't care, they didn't care about me at all. They only cared about what I could do for them, what I could give them, it was all about them the entire time.

That's one of the things you have to worry about. When you meet someone, you have to worry about whether they're real or not. From the beginning, they showed me who they were, but I chose to ignore it. Pay attention to all the signs that people give you, they are there, you just need to make sure that you're looking, listening, and watching.

CHAPTER 2:

I FORGIVE YOU

I forgive you, I am letting you know that I forgive you, that I have let you into my life for a period of time and did not decide to take it back. You made me feel like you only wanted me for what I had, not for who I am. I expressed my love for you and you didn't reciprocate nor appreciate it. Your only response was, "I care about you", but then there were several times where you would go out, and party hang out leaving me at home alone.

I forgive you for that, getting a drunk call, cussing me out, telling me that you don't want me and you don't want to be with me. You said you were only using me, but for some reason when we spoke the next day, you forgot all of what you said, so yeah, I forgive you.

I forgive you for wanting to be in my life, but not knowing how to handle someone like me, in your life. You thought you could treat me anyway that you wanted to, in any way that you could, but I showed up. Not only did I show up, you realized that I'm not that type of person, and I'm definitely not that guy, so I forgive you for not knowing.

I forgive you for creating an area in my life where I really was emotionally in trouble, but yet you took advantage of my heart. By trying to help me emotionally, sexually and physically by trying to make me forget why my heart was hurting, but I woke up. Then I realized that the pain was still there and it could only be removed through the help of God, not a man, so yeah, I forgive you.

I forgive you for pretending to care, pretending to love me, pretending to make me feel like I was that one. Pretending that you could be with me, but yet you were with others. But what you didn't realize was that I already knew. The late calls, the sudden change in your tone, the way you smelled when you came home. Like in true nature of me I forgave you, persuaded myself like it never happened, but then I met one of them, and of course, I forgive you for it.

I forgive you because you did not know how to express yourself when it came to me. You did not know how to express how you were feeling. You just let it lingered and wandered around "trying to figure things out", which is what you said. Which would hurt me deep inside, because you only had to say three little words, "Let's take a break". So yeah, I forgive you.

I forgive you for telling me what I wanted to hear, instead of telling me what I should be hearing from you. You should have told me how you really felt. That was what you really wanted from me, was just to be friends. I could have accepted that, but you just dragged it on like you really wanted to be with me. I mean the entire time, you knew that you couldn't love me or be with me, not that it was hard to forgive you for but I did.

I forgive you for calling me afterward, and I basically told you that I want nothing to do with you anymore. I decided I was just going to move on without you. Even after I blocked you, even after you deleted me from social media as your friend, but yet you still like my pictures, you still like everything I did. You still tried to talk to me, sending me messages like "I really wish you would talk to me". No, I'm not going to talk to you. I forgave you, only because you were trying to communicate with me after I told you that I did not want to talk to you any longer.

You continuously tried to make time and take up space in my life when you knew that you didn't want to either. You realized that who I was and whom I was going to become and you wanted to be a part of it, you could never reciprocate, I just let you go and to this day I still don't want it back. I forgive you for that. Because you challenged me to look deep within myself and get to see the real me, I say thank you.

I need you to forgive me because I should have known better but most of all I need you to forgive me for giving you and showing you my love that was honest, true and you didn't deserve it from me. Please forgive me. I must say there is always two sides of the story so I need you to forgive me, I allowed you to be the way you were with me even though I had already known the outcome. I need you to forgive me for letting you take advantage of me, pulling me into situations that I knew were no good for me. Using my feelings against me to get what you wanted. I also need you to forgive me for being there when you needed me, for taking care of you when you needed to be taken care of. I also need you to forgive me for showing you true love, true friendship, even though that was never your intentions.

Forgive me for all the negative thoughts that I had, those that I knew could hurt you physically and emotionally. My thoughts would hurt you if I told you how I felt, words that would crush you. If I told you how I felt, they would even make me cry just thinking about them.

Forgive me because I don't think that you're really a part of me like I'm apart of yours, and for every time I turn around, I wanted your love, your attention, your gift of friendship, your affection that you could not even give me. I allowed you to come into my life and just take, from me without given me nothing in return but a bill. A heavy price tag of our friendship. Never a word of encouragement. Have you ever thought maybe I needed that sometimes? Forgive me for saying, that I should be forgiving myself for allowing all of this to just show up in my life.

Forgive me for being there for you when you needed me, for checking on you when you need it to be checked on. Seems to me that I was there for your attention and not mine. I ask for your forgiveness for caring for you, for always being in your corner, having your back. Knowing that sooner or later you would need me again and I would be there for you like I always do.

Things just aren't equal, I'm running to you but you steadily pushing me away. I'm always showing you that I have hopes and dreams; and all you can see dollar signs. I was the one telling you to hang in there, and that you could be whatever you wanted, that was me.

Please forgive me, for all of that because of the way I see it. I'm the one that needs to forgive you or is it you that should be forgiven me? You should forgive me for caring and you're not caring. You should be forgiving me for loving you though you're not showing me you love in return. You should be forgiving me for me being in your corner and you sometimes seem like you could care less one way or another. What I got from you were not responses to love, you show me that you didn't care. But what I did get out of you was whatever you could get out of me for free. This has been your response to everything. Let me tell you how to start rebuilding yourself.

First, forgive yourself for treating you the way that you did. I don't think you will ever go anywhere if you don't. You might not ever get anything off the ground unless you forgive yourself. Please know whatever decision you choose is a direct reflection on how your life will turn out if you move forward with an unforgiving heart. You sometimes have to quiver and be shook to your core, so you can be brought to your knees.

Forgiveness and success work together. This shouldn't surprise you. If you hold onto your hurt and resentment you can never get to where you are supposed to be. When you choose to let go of the hurt you are freeing yourself. When you forgive someone that has wronged you is very powerful. No one said it would be easy, it's actually harder than you think. Choosing forgiveness can be one of the most difficult things to do, but also can be a rewarding decision if done correctly. But at the end of the day don't find yourself trying to figure out how to forgive, when you have already been forgiven.

CHAPTER 3:

Have you ever

Have you ever been in love with someone who just sweeps you off your feet? They literally take your breath away, makes you smile at the sound or mere thought of their name. When they are not around you easily miss them, you always wish they were standing in front of you or sitting next to you. When you are with them the air quality changes because you are breathing for each other, usually this happens when you fall in love with someone.

At this point, I'm not quite sure if I'm in love or if I'm in like. I love the way they make me feel, the way they make me laugh, and smile. I mean, I love that they can hold a conversation they have a lot of interesting things to say. I sometimes feel like they are basically a simple person and that they don't want or need a lot. Lately, they have expressed that they just want himself and now he's told me that he wants me. That's the way love goes, well then so be it.

The problem with a lot of relationships and a lot of the ways people handle things is they sitting around waiting on someone to call them all the time. When all they have to do is pick the phone up and call that person to see what's going on or to see how they're doing or to see what's up for tonight.

The other problem with that is you always realize it the very next day, "I thought you were going to call me last night", or "oh thank you so much for calling me last night when you said you were going to", the best one is "thank you for calling me and it's been two or three days". Now the solution sinks in. The phone works both ways you don't have to wait around for somebody to call you. You should be able to pick that phone up and make a call for yourself. Stop waiting around for people to call you.

I don't understand what it is now that we have to sit around and wait for people to call. Maybe one feels like they are calling too much and wants to give the other person a chance to call. Now if this is you, don't get mad because this is what you asked for. All because you asked for them to give you a chance to call, they gave you just that, several chances for you to call. Now the phone calls have come to almost a halt and you cannot handle what you asked for. Be careful what you wish for.

Now you are all in your feelings with an attitude, the very next day "Oh, thank you for calling me" or "Why didn't you call me," or "Where have you been?" If you had picked up the phone like you use to, you would have to know what was going on the other end. Instead, you decided to wait for me to call you, sitting there by the phone all night worried about what's going on, try picking up the phone and try calling yourself. After all, you said you wanted the opportunity to call more often. Now, who does that sound like?

I've been swept off my feet several times I remember the first time when I was dating, you have to be careful with eye candy because sometimes that is just what it is, eye candy. I was fresh out the military I thought they were the sexiest person I've ever met in my life. We kept in touch with each other. I would go meet them at the gate, go to their house to spend the weekend. I always enjoy the weekend however, their neighbor across the street was just as fine they flirted with me every weekend. The flirting became so bold that, my friend was told I'm going to have your man. They argued and came to an agreement not to have those discussions again because them having me was not going to happen.

I was sitting outside when they apologize to each other. Later on, the neighbor decides to walk across the yard and sit down beside me just started talking and touching me and rubbing my legs, and I said "I would advise you not to do that" and they asked "Oh, what if I don't? Not knowing my friend watched the entire thing from the window and how I was touched should only be by someone special. I got up, did what I had to do to get them off me. I made sure that it would never happen again. I got up and went into the house and that's when my friend grabbed me to bring me in closer and proceeded to kiss me and say, "I love you because I knew you would never cheat on me" I was confused, so I asked "Did you send them out there?" they responded "Yes, I did I asked them why. They told me a test had to be given, I told them they would never have to test me because I'm not that kind of guy that needs to be tested." Needless to say, when I got back to the house I took all my things, that was truly a sign of things to come, and a true sign that they had trust issues. They tried to apologize but none was needed at all. I let them know that the next guy, you decide to test, make sure you have a made up mind to handle the repercussions of their response. Not everyone will put up with certain things that I did, not everyone is understanding and kind.

CHAPTER 4:

I QUIT!!!
(THE DATING GAME)

Dating now has really changed. I mean you practically have to fill out an application for dating. It has really come to that. Maybe I really just need to find someone in another state, another country. Or just maybe another planet, because this is not getting it at all.

The problem with it all is, that everyone is looking for the perfect guy, or the perfect girl still in 2019; we are still looking for perfect. That's not going to happen. When you say perfect, there are so many aspects to being perfect, straight hair, but now they do natural, straight teeth, just let them be white, the one that really is a good eye-catcher, of course, excellent credit. Who needs good credit in today's society to date, get your own credit fixed? Not everyone is going to be the perfect picture. Just find the person you can cuddle, kiss, hold the romantic stuff that comes with dating for the first 30 days and you will be able to know just who you are dating.

Back to the application part of it, dating is actually like a job. You fill out the application and wait to see if you are a match, there's the dating part, the getting to know you phase, as I like to call it. Most application have questions like: Are you a virgin? How many sexual partners have you had in the last 2, 4, 10 years? Do you smoke or drink, social or habitually? Your education level or Do you have a mental illness? Have you ever cheated on a previous partner? Why should I date you? And my most favorite, list any specialty you may have that is relevant to our proposed relationship? What, really is this what we have come to?

Can we just go back to regular dating each other like movies and dinner, talking and getting to know one another? There has to be a time when you say enough is enough with all these question and answers just to say hi.

Take, for instance, I met someone in November of 2011, we starting dating and getting to know each other, we went to the movies turns out they were just as much of a kid at heart like I was. Dinner was great we both had a lot to say. Long walks loved them as much as I did. Everything was going great. Remember to do your homework.

Thanksgiving went by and we did not spend it together and that was okay with me. Christmas came, I spent it at home with my family. We kept in contact during the holidays and talked, laughed and listen to each other breathing on the phone as you do as teenagers. Once I returned from visiting with my family for the holidays, things got a little weird. I didn't see them as much nor did I talk to them as much.

I decided to go to their church, they always invited me too. I decided to surprise them. I was the one with the surprise handed to me. This particular Sunday I choose to get to the service, unknowingly to me it was an appreciation service for none other than the pastor and their beautiful family. It appeared to include two lovely daughters who had to be at least 14 and 20 years of age. I sat in the back of the church and watch and listen to the service, ironically enough, the sermon speaking on "The Family". Well, needless to say, in the middle of the service, I stood up and walked out making sure they saw me. I did get a text message "Boo, please let me explain".

Explain what, how you made me feel like a fool, how I thought I was the only one or better yet, I was the only one. Technically, when I was told they were not dating anyone else they didn't lie, instead, they were married. That's called a half-truth for the young readers. It's never a good feeling when you have been betrayed by anyone yet especially someone married. I thought the days of what you don't know won't hurt you, but yet they are still alive and well. I decided then to just QUIT and never date again. Being hurt, deceived and betrayed is not a good feeling for anyone I don't care who you are. I think that dating in this era is going to be one of the toughest challenges an older single person will have.

Back when I was younger it was as easy as, "Do you like me check yes or no and slide it back into my locker". Those were the days when dating as easy, getting turned down was okay, being rejected didn't matter because nothing at the age was etched into stone. There was always someone interested in you when you were not even interested in them.

Needless to say, I did date again a few months went by and I met another nice person, they were sweet kind and very attractive. I was asked if I wanted to out on a date and get to know them, agreed with some hesitation. I didn't understand, but I did. We decided to meet the next day at a restaurant. I got there about 10 minutes early, to watch them walk in, however they had the same idea. I got seated shortly after I walked in, they came in along with a friend of theirs. We spoke, greeted each other and they left for a few minutes. Long story short, they had brought another friend to meet me, because they weren't the one interested in me, the friend was and surprisingly shy.

We began to talk and getting to know each other eventually, the meeting planner disappeared and just faded into the background. As we continued to talk, I noticed that they were as shy as they said, glaring and staring at others walking into the restaurant. They excused himself to the bathroom but hooked up with another in the bathroom hall for a kiss. Needless to say, when they returned to the table I was gone. Never let a pretty face fool you, they don't fool me for a bit, and that shy routine, I am shy, I know what being shy looks like. So again. I QUIT, I give up on dating, finding the right love, finding the person to love me back and to have my back.

I was beginning to see just how people are and who they were. To play their part and their games were not for me. I was truly done this time. I was not trying to hear that any more. I talked to many people so I can get to make new friends and learning the ways of people. I actually ran into an old friend that we tried to talk before but now seems to have come to his senses, it was the summer of 2012.

We first met on a dating line, and they did not know what I looked like until we met. I drove to see them and it was pretty nice. We had learned a lot about each other over the phone, but when we finally met in person it solidified what we have felt for each other, I know young love right? We had spent the entire day together getting to know each other, we went to dinner, the movies and we just drove around talking. Finally, it was time we ended the day. We had connected for several months before we decided this was what we were going to do. We spend birthdays together, holidays together and even just because we missed each other type of days.

I had begun to see a change in him about three years into the relationship. I would often ask if they loved me and of course, I was told yes, but I have never thought about asking if they were in love with me. You would have thought I learned from the last time it happened. Never had I even thought or imagined that someone could love you and not be in love with you. The holidays we use to spend with each other were no longer that important, my birthday was forgotten while theirs was remembered and even just because days were even dwindling away. Finally, they came to the house I was excited to see them but they were drunk. Have you ever had the one drunk person to get on your nerves so bad that you just wanted to throw them out of a window, well I did? Well, dropped them out of the window, I did dangle their feet for about 5 min before I let them go. Besides they were only 2 feet from the ground, to a drunk person dangling out of the window that is like 20 feet. They started fussing and cussing and I laughed. They got mad and drove their drunk self-home. They could have stayed the night but, didn't want to because I am the evil one. I knew right then and there I was not going to let anyone take me out of my comfort zone. Yet again, I QUIT dating. I was giving up because dating was getting more and more hopeless, or was I just attracting the wrong people?

When you meet certain people, you try to feel them out for yourself some are timid and shy. You really want to be with them but because of who they are you don't know what to expect. It's not usual for me to date the same type of person back to back but it happens. They both were short, both worked in the medical field, thick and chubby, and attractive the only thing is that they both lived in two different cities. Dating both of them was the same as all the others, dinner, movies spending time at parks, the beach, they both partied and I did not, they were the same age born under the same sign. Another difference between both of them was when they love they hold back, not giving and showing their true feelings for the person they are with. This makes it difficult for them to be with anyone, or to trust themselves or with anyone else for that matter to do the right thing when it comes to being in a relationship with them. I would find myself making the moves and choosing everything that we did, but when it came to them making a decision it was always strategically as in what's in it for me. These people have to be the hardest people to ever date. Sometimes it's all about them and sometimes it's not. The quiet ones are always thinking.

Someone asked me if I have ever dated someone that fights. Of course, I have dated somebody for approximately 8 months before…., well let me explain. You are who you attract, I think that rule does not apply to me. I have attracted some drunks, I don't drink, smokers and I don't smoke and weed heads and I definitely don't do that. I can say I have attracted some loving, kind and caring people as well just not in my state. It has been a trying time dating people.

I met them in a bar, he seemed to be a nice guy. He was attractive kind and very intelligent. We went to the movies, dinners, we traveled and had a great time together. It's just that his drinking at times, was out of control. I could be home and would get a call they were crying and begging me to come over, of course after dealing with previous drunks I did not. They would threaten to kill themselves, but somehow miraculously they would be alive the next morning. Many times, we would have yelling fights and shouting over the phone but when we got around each other they would always apologize. The day of our break up I was at their house watching TV on the couch and they were drinking, they finally joined me on the couch and laid on me. I moved because they stink and I told them. That's when the shouting started.

Now mind you they were 6 feet tall and very slim. I was 6ft 3in tall and average build. When they moved to where I was, I tried to move again when I felt a hard hand across the back of my head. I advised them to take a nap, they did after two more beers. I got the duct tape, and the rope tied their feet and hands together and duct taped them all together, by this time they were waking up I took them to the bathroom put him in the tub and turned the water on. Of course, there was a drain and it was open.

Remember drunk people will believe any kind of fear when they are drunk. They tried to get loose but have you ever seen a turtle on its back? That is what it looked like. I packed up my belongs that I had at their place. Got them together to call a family member. Spoke with his brother and provided him with an updated of his condition and his brother agreed to come by and check on him. He did and called to tell me maybe they will know how to treat the next one. I never heard from them again. Now being with someone like that would make anyone QUIT and never think about dating again.

I have dated a slick mouth talker before however, the very brief romantic dating of 18-months thing we had. Early on, I was ready to quit them, but people can change so I thought. Right from the start, they seemed like they were the type that could get over on you or at least try to get over on you. We met in a café, in Seattle. They used the pick-up line of all pickup lines. "I have a headache from looking at such a handsome man as you, blah, blah, blah, but I found it cute.

Dating this one was different they could be sweet at times and then turn into a, for lack of better words monster. I often found myself dating myself with them. We would plan to go out but would always have an excuse, instead of an excuse they could have said they were broke. But I always came to the rescue and say this one is on me. Well, you can get tired of saying this one's on me and I did. This caused several fights especially when they started to demand that I pay for dinner and movie. This was the first relationship I actually had to hit someone. I am not saying hitting someone is okay, but in a matter of life and death, knock them out. We tore that room up, their place of course. Somehow, I managed not to get a scratch on me. At this point, I had decided to leave this relationship or Quit. Sometimes it is a good thing to quit and give up, it just depends on what you are quitting, or who you are quitting on, or who had quit on you.

I have been quitted on, yes me sweet, kind loveable me. I was in love with them, yes, I was. We dated, shopped, went for walks in the park, dinner, and movies. I met the family. I cared so much for them and they were my everything. This was in the early Nineties. It was unexpected, very beautiful, long dark hair. My family had seen pictures of them, they talked to them on the phone and we were on the road to getting married. Every day I would go to lunch with them. We worked across the street from each other. I was called their "Prince Charming". We went to church together, we did everything together. I guess I knew they would definitely be the one to change me.

It was a Friday, I had to go out of town for a business meeting. We talked every night and as much as we could during the day for three days. They had a best friend that never wanted to see them happy. This friend did not like me. They found that this was the perfect opportunity to split us up. They were the type that believed everything people told them. Their friend had found out that I was out of town and decided to fill their head with ideas of where I was or was not, so once I got back, we had planned to meet. We spoke on the phone and I was called a liar, a cheat and a dog. I had no clue what they were talking about. I went to their house, they were not home from work but their mom was there. Their mom asked me to tell her the truth, where was I. I actually show their mom the truth, the hotel bill, the receipts, meeting schedule and airlines ticket stubs.

They saw me when they can home and was immediately outraged, threw the ring at me, we were 4 months from being married. Their mom tried to stop them but in my mind, it was over. I took the ring and left. Later they called and apologized because their mom told them the truth, I was not going back to them, I was not about to go through that again. Needless to say, they stopped believing everything people told them. See when someone quits you it's different.

Sometimes it takes a dose of the reality of what you are actually giving up on when you quit things. However, many of us believe that this is the best option. If you can't win, quit. If you can't get ahead, just quit. No job promotion quit. I often think about quitting my job, dating and just deal with me. Just be with me, myself, and simply just giving up on the possibility of having anyone else in my life.

Quitting is easy to do, but what becomes of a quitter, I'll tell you, you turn out to be that lady with a thousand cats or the troll under the bridge. Why, bother having someone else in your life that is going to disappoint you when you can just disappoint yourself and try to live, be happy and content with that.

So, go ahead and quit. Quit your family, because they don't love and support you, quit your friends, because it seems like they are never there, quit your church, because they don't care about you either, they don't check on you like they are supposed to, they only know you, when you don't pay your tithes, quit everything. Quit the whole world, because that is what you are really saying. Better yet, quit yourself, because, in the end, this is what you are really doing, giving up on everything including yourself and all possibilities of being happy.

CHAPTER 5:
SO WHAT HAPPENS NOW?

You are at this point in your life where there is literally, no one out there that will actually meet what you're looking for. After you've been to the point where you know how to love, know how to accept love, know how to give and receive love there's no going back to anything else. You won't accept anything less. When a person you love, becomes your everything. You learn to love them through everything, the hurt, the pain, the heartache, the yelling the screaming and crying, when I say everything, I mean everything. You know they become your love, and you just can't treat it like it's whatever, you have to treat love the way it deserves to be treated. And it consumes your mind body and soul, to make you feel like you are the whole person God intended you to be, but when it's lost, how do you come back from that?

This is what you do, you pray, and pray some more. It's going to take more than prayer to get through this one.

Trying to search to find the right person to be with. You date one and they mostly talk about sex and you really don't need that in your life right now. Then you date another one and they're about the same thing and then you try to keep searching until finding the one. You talk for days, you talk for weeks and then talk for months and finally have that sex and it's over with, which is what they were looking for all along. Most people are afraid to say what they mean, and mean what they say. They are afraid of rejection. A lot of people today won't tell you what they want up front, they will wait for you to try to guess what they want. Dating or getting to know someone is not a guessing game.

Put your cards on the table, it's a whole lot easier that way. There are times when you know you just want to be held, you just want to be cuddled, whatever happened to the intimacy with no sex, whatever happened to the walks in the park or the drives for no reason, sitting on the beach listening to the waves crash against the rocks, or the walks that you used to take just walking down the street holding hands, holding each other smiling at each other. These are the things that build relationship character, you don't see that anymore those days have long gone so you have to find a new way to love yourself, physically, mentally and emotionally.

Show whomever it is what you're looking for because if you don't show them, they'll never know.

Once you find that love, what do you do with it? Embrace it, but don't smother it, you hold it, you fight for it. You get through pain with it, you push through it. Love is not easy, it is not easy at all when I was married. There were days where I didn't think we were going to make it, but we did just a little stuff that just irritated me, little things about me too irritated them. We live through it and we loved through it. We made sure we did not go to bed at night without saying we love each other. It mattered to us that love had to matter, and it has to love.

Love has to have a reason, love has to have someone to water it and someone to make it grow. Love is a partnership, you have to be together you have to be in sync, your thoughts combined will do things before it can even be thought of, and you will wonder how the other person even knew. Love has to have a purpose, a reason to exist, just a reason to thrive, a reason to live, without one of those reasons love is going to die.

Don't get stuck, because when you do, you'll be stuck in the same spot that you were in before you found that love. Depending on how long you were together the game has changed and the rules have changed. It's going to be hard to try to find somebody to love you the way that individual did.

When you get this love, this new love you have to remember don't make them pay for what you've been through, don't make them pay for what you were lacking, don't make them pay for what you needed in the last relationship. And another thing, once you have that love, feel it out, get to know what it's like to be loved, to know what it's like to be in love. The next person will have to love you their own way, they will have to be in love with you their own way, and you have to accept that you cannot compare apples to oranges. You just have to accept the fact that everybody loves differently but you have to remember what it feels like to love. Hold on to the love you have, cherish it, nurture it, squeeze it as tight as you can, don't ever let it go because once you do, it's gone forever.

CHAPTER 6:
COMMUNICATION

There's a lot of talk about what people want in relationships, one of the main key things that people express and want is the 3 C's. Commitment, communication, clarity, but the one thing that really gets everybody in trouble is the communication part.

When we begin to talk about what we want in a partnership or in a lasting relationship a lot of people's main request is communication.

Yes, communication is the key but it should never be one-sided. The phrase "the phone works both ways" has a meaning. Text messaging included, we all understand that we do get busy. But however, it doesn't mean I'm going to sit by the phone for the next three days waiting for you to text or to call me after I have already text and called you.

Let me make this personal for you, see I noticed, that you have time to sit on Facebook, that you have time to sit on Twitter. I even noticed that you have time to post on Instagram, LinkedIn and all the other social media sites but it's been 2 days since I have text or call you. I don't have any response from you so that's basically telling me to move on and that you are too busy to text, call or send a smoke signal, perhaps you don't know how to say "I'm not interested", play the card, let's just be friends. Personally, I would take either than nothing at all.

The reality is, that's just how some people are, they do not know how to communicate without getting their feelings involved or at least be courteous enough to tell the other party you are not interested. But the way people look at it is if you got time to do all this posting everywhere else but you don't have time to pick the phone up and call the one that you so called want to be with. Or the one you want to date.

This is why your phone number has been deleted, you've been deleted off of Facebook and all other social media platforms that we used to communicate on. Then you just happen to call or text, and you get met with the "who is this?" that's why. Now don't try to explain yourself, or save face with the "oh I was busy," because we already know you were not. Now here's a couple of clues or a couple of ideas on things that you might want to do or invest your life in order to be with the person that you claim that you want to be with.

Number one be consistent in either calling or texting daily, it's going to take some work. Perhaps, send a smoke signal, throw a rock at a window, or a drive-by daily text. Do something daily to let them know that you are still breathing, that you are still around that you still want them, and you care. Seriously, it doesn't matter just do something daily if you forget, call them the next day but don't let two or three days go by.

Number two show them and let them know that you care. Plan a movie night or day with them, take them to dinner. Try to go to their house, call first, let them know you want to come over and spend time. Or, I'm coming over I'm going to pick you up, we just going to go for a ride. Just talk or go sit somewhere, in the park. Watch the sun go down over the lake, or something, don't let it always be just a conversation over the phone.

Number three you say you love this person, you say you want to be with this person, the catch is you live 600 plus miles away, or even an hour. Distance plays a major part in a relationship and you will need to put forth the effort to communicate more frequently. It's easy for people to lose interest when there is no communication or not enough.

Again, make the effort or the attempt to see each other at least once a month, especially if you are far away from each other. Now if that's too much for you, try every two months and don't always let it be one-sided you go see them they come to you. There are plenty of opportunities and ways that you can see each other better yet, Face time with each other at least two or three times a week to let them know that you're interested and that you really are trying to be there and want to see them.

When love is lost, it's gone. You can try to get it back but it takes work. Keep it fresh daily. Talk to each other, listen to each other. Don't talk at or listen to, talk to and listen to. No sense in trying to get it me back if you for one minute, make me feel like you don't want me. Trust me it happens, the "I feel you don't want me." I'm pretty much sure it has happened to a lot of people, and I am reassuring you that is does.

Another important sign that communication is heavy between the two of you is when you just go on about your day and you think about this person and the phone rings and it's them. When they are calling you out of the normal time when you talk to each other. If you ask them, what makes you call me this time of day, and their answer is because you're on my mind. When you can't get off the phone with them no matter how hard you try because you are working, and don't want to hang up with them but you know you got to get back to work so then you hang up with them only to realize that the whole time that they were calling you they were right outside your job, just coming to take you to lunch. These are the kind of relationships we strive for. Communication will get you to these places in your life.

Sometimes in the relationships that we are in, or the friendships, partnerships, BFF, cuddle buddies or just plain friends, whatever kind of relationship it is we sometimes get lost along the way. Lost in ourselves, the other person, work, school, and the list go on but the main person other than ourselves is discarded by the road and we forgot to go back and pick them up. Somehow by thinking about ourselves and not thinking about how the other person's feeling. The communication line gets dropped.

Communication has many different forms. Yes, thinking about a person, means you are connected by another level. But you need to act on that thought you are having.

This is how you know when you are with the right person. When you go to bed at night they're the last person you talk to and when you wake up in the morning sometimes, other than God, because He is first, they're either the first person you talk to or the first person that comes across your mind.

You can't go throughout the day without thinking about this person. Every time you think about them you smile every time the phone rings whether it's them or not you smile.

The other way that you know that you really like this person is you are in a conversation with one of your best friends and everybody that you see walk past you, you think it's them. You can't concentrate, you can't sleep with talking to them at night, you get mad when they do not call, and when you do hear from them, they apologize and you say, no problem.

This means that you have the communication part down

and you know when to expect to hear from them. You are ready and willing, and able to hear from them because you are going to give them the same communication back.

It happens, and then this is how you know you really, really like that person. You sit at your desk and you just writing their name over and over just like you did in junior high school. By now you have communication down, they are mentally in your head. You can't wait to hear from them or see them, it makes you anxious about seeing them the next time or talking to them. When you hear their voice it makes you melt, makes you float to another planet or among the clouds. You forget what time of the day it is and where you are sometimes. Most people say this is love or infatuation, but you have to remember how got you to this place. It all started with the communication of two people expressing an interest in each other. Without those first few words, glances, the hi, or the hello you would have not made it this far.

Take it from me there are lots of ways that you can break communication and ruin the relationship. The ones that you knew you were supposed to be with for rest of your life, with that person and there's no way to get it back. Please, keep the lines of communication open. Call that person, go by and see that person, send them smoke screens, throw rocks at the windows, drive by the house, knock on their door, leave a note and run, do what you got to do to make it playful, loving and lasting to let them know that you care. Show them you want to be in their life. Allow you actions to speak volumes on your behalf. Go fly a kite with yours and their name on it. Just do something to keep those lines of communication open just to be with the one that you want to be with.

CHAPTER 7:

A Ray of hope

There is always a reason to not throw in the towel in just yet. Sometimes when you feel like you just want to quit and be done with everyone and everything. Someone comes along and makes your day. There are a lot of reasons to not quit, and give up and yes love is one of them or the hope of love should I say. You can find reasons to not quit anywhere as I did even in the grocery store.

I was in the grocery store minding my own business, I saw someone looking at me from the corner of my eye. I smile and they saw me. Asked me my name and we began to talk. I wasn't long before we began to talk every day and spent time together. This was when I would doubt myself about dating them or anyone. There were times that I would question my feelings because this was all new to me again. After all my spouse had now been deceased two years almost. So of course, I am naturally going to feel this way. We talked about my life and their life, we talked even more about all that I have been through of losing my spouse. (This shows you that they cares and is concerned about your feelings).

Often times, we would go to dinner choosing every other time of where we would go until the day, they chose their kitchen. Impressive I thought. The movies were the same, we took turns choosing them. Spending time with them became easy for me. The holidays were perfect, spending them with them was unforgettable. The countryside drives we had, the meeting of their friends and family meant a lot to me. I was really being shown just how much I was cared for.

We had late-night calls where we would listen to each other snore before we said good night. The laughter, the tv shows that we share and have in common. Most day while we work, we text each other and little odd and end messages. The mid-day lunch dates are really great. Going out for night walks and long drives in the city. When we spend time with our friends apart from each other we try not to call, but that was a failure at its best we wanted to hear from each other.

At this point they truly know me, they know how I am feeling about something, and they are usually right on. I don't know how they do it, but I am glad they can. I have never felt so happy, elated alive and full of hope. It feels like the stars light up for me at night when I think of them. I mean, who could ask for more, right?

Sometimes when we do not talk to each other, it drives me crazy as I want to know who they are with, what they are doing. And why haven't they called me? I have to remember that they have friends and had a life before I came into the picture, and a family even though I have met them. I am learning to be patient with matter. You have to give them their space to be themselves. Not to mess up but to just be who they really are with the knowledge and understanding you are enough for them. If you are not, time will tell.

For the most part, learning to be in a relationship can be difficult depending on the person you choose.

In the new era of dating it's almost like we have to relearn how to date, to talk and to have fun without the preconceived ideas in the back of our minds that they are going to leave us for someone else. Or, they are going to leave us because we do not make them happy. Sometimes we feel like, either we are smothering them or they are smothering us, but we are afraid to talk about it due to us not wanting to get out feelings hurt. Remember it's a process and you can not allow your insecurities to take over your thoughts, let alone the discussions. Now that we are always in our feelings, only because we have been in relationships the lasted for years and now, we find ourselves alone again and trying to date in the new millennium.

We find ourselves rushing to say I love you and marrying people that we don't truly know, just so we won't be alone, that is something we need to quit.

I am not saying go out and find that man or find that woman that makes you happy for right now, but find that one you want to be the last one, the last relationship, or the one you know just can't live without. They are your air, they are you sun in the morning, your moon and night even as cliché as it may sound the butter on your toast, or the cream in your coffee. Life is too short to be dealing with other problems, and their foolishness. Find that one that makes you happy, the one that makes you smile and the one that makes you remember what love is about and how love can truly make you feel, and that makes you never want to quit.

However, there are times when I wonder, am I what they are looking for and are they what I need in my life?

Only time will tell, and I'll keep you posted….

ABOUT THE AUTHOR

James-Deric Newkirk aka "Deric" is the founder and CEO of U'Neekly D'Zigned Jewelry. Born and raised in a little town called Atkinson, North Carolina he has always had a flair for writing music, poetry, short stories. In school he used to write his own comic books for class projects. He has always wrote poetry, eventually he was to follow his passion of writing as well as jewelry making not being able to choose between the two he decided to do both.

James has always had a business mindset, of crafting, and writing. It wasn't until the loss of his spouse in 2017 that he realized that he has a lot of his own life stories and grief and history to share with others. He began writing passionately in journals on napkins, scrap paper whatever he has in his hand. He kept a journal beside his bed and just wrote constantly writing about his life, things he saw things he heard, never planning to do anything with them until he had the opportunity. After the passing of his spouse he decided not to let any of his writings, jewelry designs, not his art of crafting to no longer to go in vain.

Deciding to leave his fulltime job, he sat down and began to work even harder that before. James stands on Faith Hope and Trust, this is not my destiny, it's just part of my itinerary, the world truly has a lot to offer and he plans to see it all.

James is also a contributing author in the bestselling booked called, Cries of a Broken Man and Screams of a Broken Woman.

Feel free to stay connected with James via social media at:

www.Facebook.com/UneeklyDzigned
www.Instagram.com/UneeklyDzigned

www.ingramcontent.com/pod-product-compliance
Lightning Source LLC
Chambersburg PA
CBHW070500050426
42449CB00012B/3066